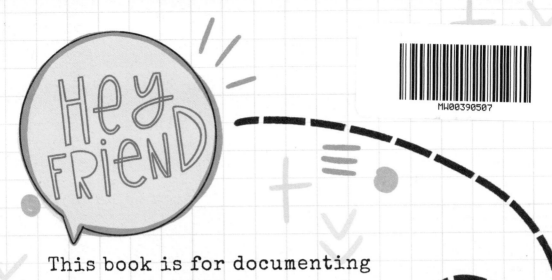

Hey Friend

This book is for documenting your faith walk in a totally personalized way! There are zero rules! Make it your own! By recording *your faith story*, you'll be able to see all the ways God is showing up for you. And at the end, you'll have a beautiful keepsake to treasure for years to come...Glue your photos, write out your *prayers*, tape in your sermon notes, scribble down your *praises*. However you want to tell your faith stories, just do it it *your* way!

SOME of MY FAVORITE SUPPLIES!!

PENS + PENCILS * stickers!

washi TAPE

RANDOM —BITS— of PAPER

PHOTOS! (get them printed!)

oh HEY! it's ME!!!

birthday

(add pic here)

i believe in

i love this
verse

loving

praying

singing

excited for

quotes
i am
loving

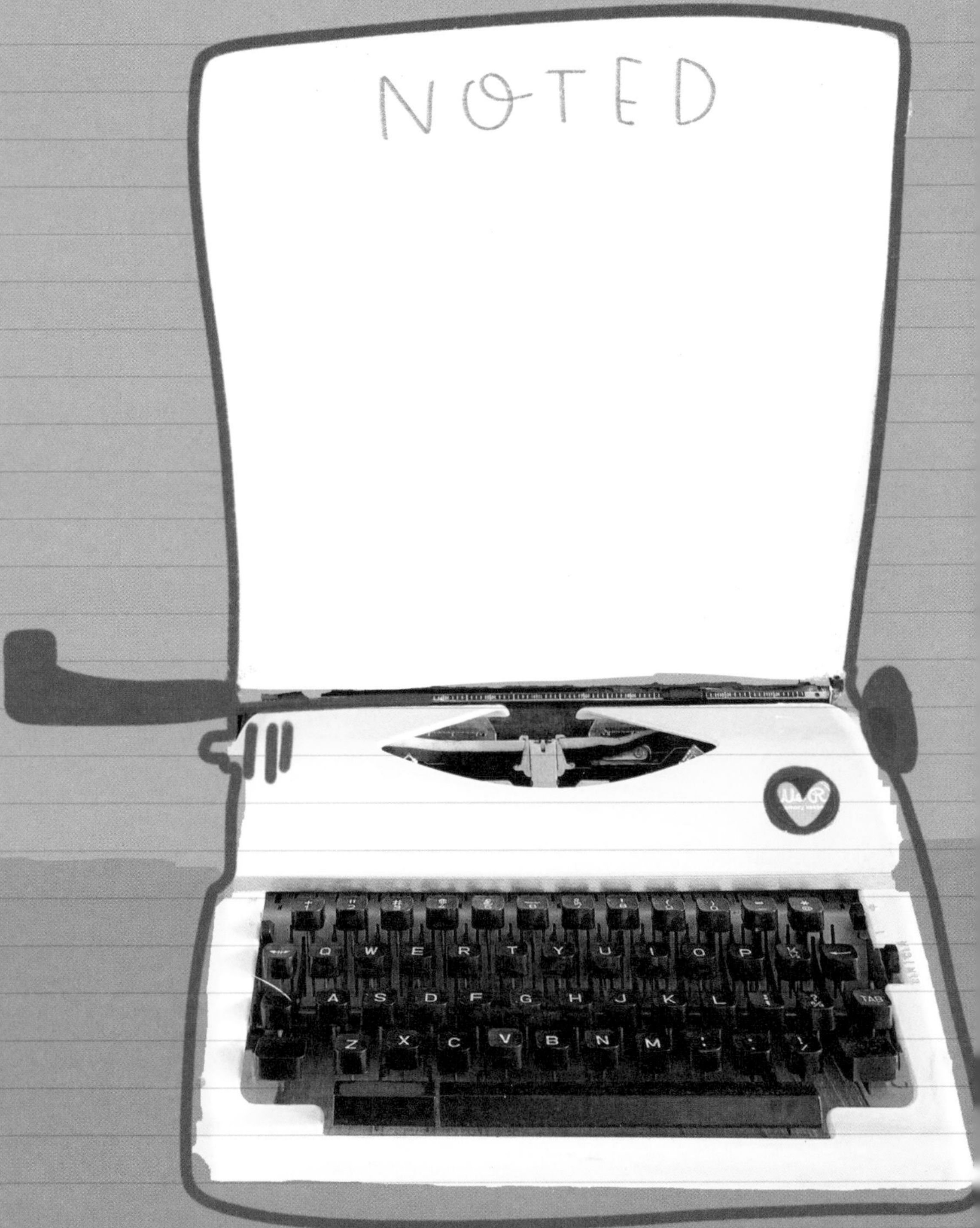
NOTED

created for purpose

HOLD FIRM IN THE TRUTH

WHERE YOU GO
I WILL GO

go

count it all joy

LYRICS

to my favorite
worship song right now

TO: GOD

SWATCHES OF THE

I ♥ MOST

_____

proof of your love

I am NOT MADE FOR FEAR!

what a
beautiful name

your
promises
are in my
heart

COVER THIS PAGE IN BEAUTIFUL PRAYERS!

little dreams
become BIG dreams
with you...

walk by faith

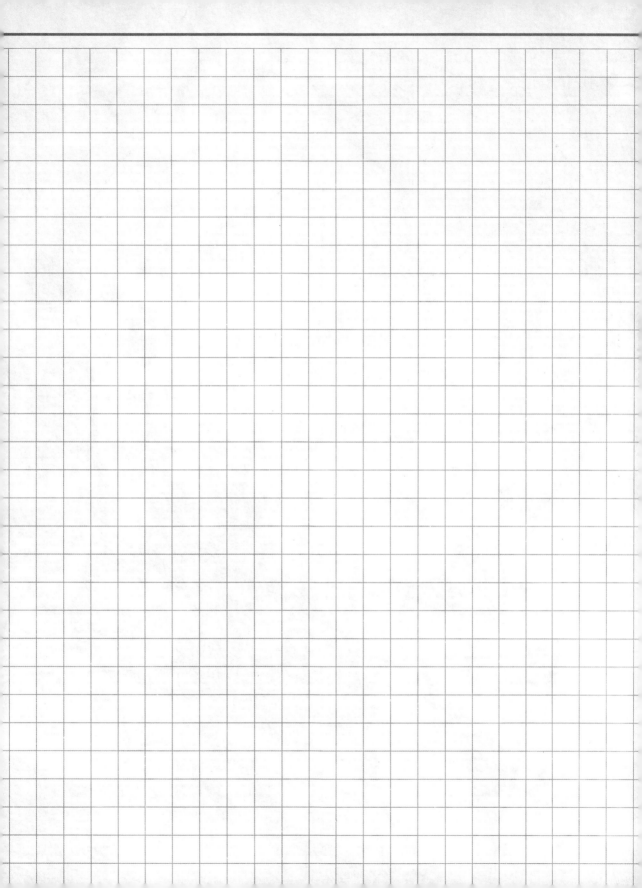

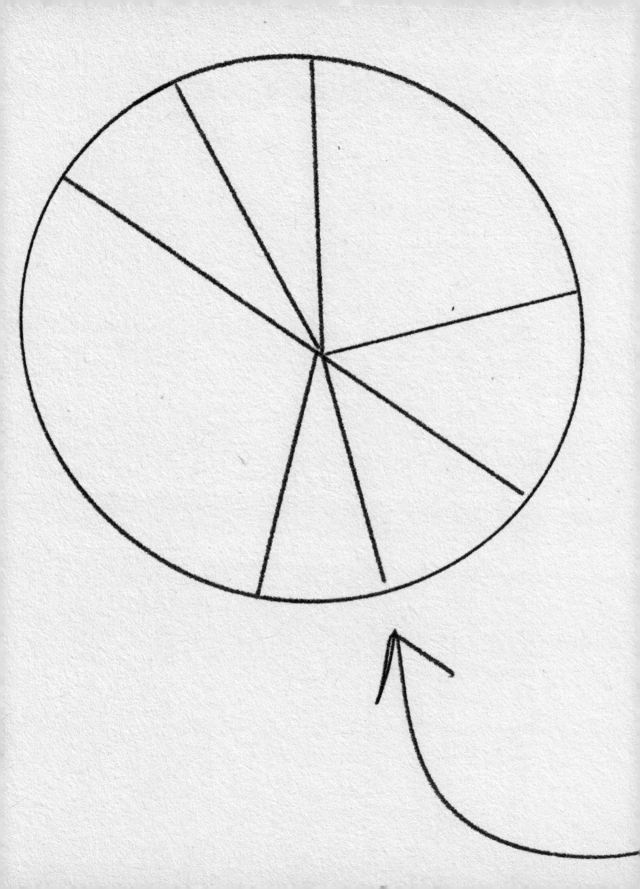

tools I USE
iN [my] FAITH

- O BIBLE STUDY
- O WORSHIP
- O PRAYER   O _____
- O _____
- O CHURCH LIFE
- O _____

COLOR CODE!

created
for glory

IS ABOUT JESUS

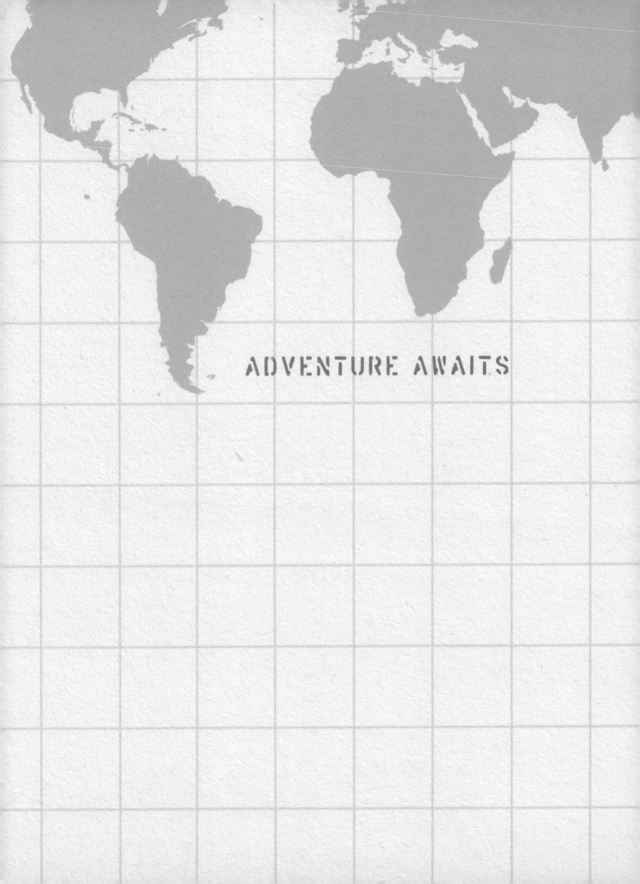

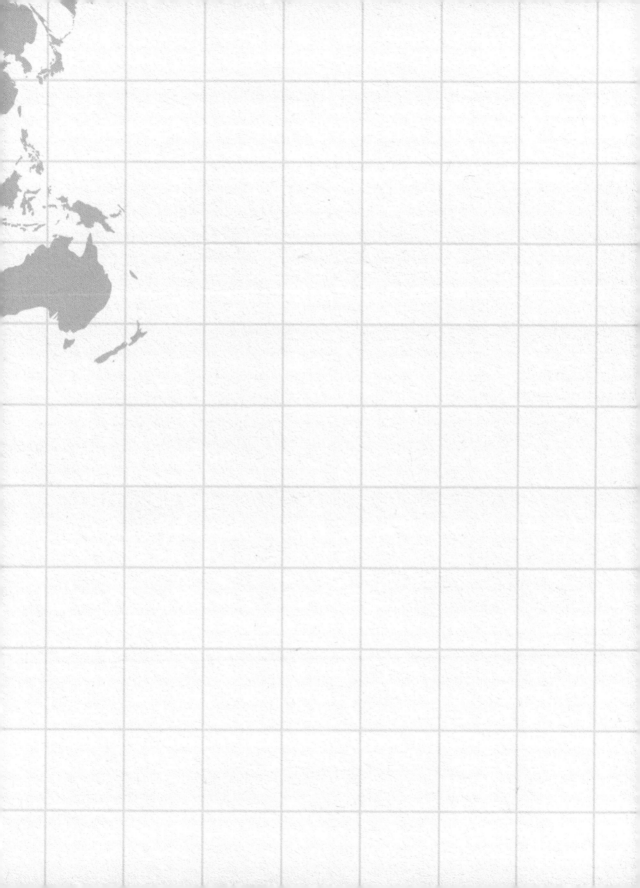

HOLY HOPE

amen

HEKI

FORGIVEN

prayers for friends

LOVE
FIRST

heaven meets earth

LOVE LIKE_____

GIVE LIKE_____

PRAY LIKE_____

LEAD LIKE_____

LEARN LIKE_____

PRAISE LIKE_____

FOLLOW LIKE_____

STUDY LIKE_____

light in

the darkness

MATTHEW 22:37–40

ALL YOUR HEART

ALL YOUR SOUL

ALL YOUR MIND

1 CHRONICLES 28:20

BE STRONG

AND COURAGEOUS

AND DO IT

GIVE THANKS

CALL ON HIS NAME

PROCLAIM HIS DEED

PROVERBS 3:5

TRUST

THE LORD

1 JOHN 3:20

GOD IS

GREATER THAN

I GIVE THANKS

TO YOU

God's love is...

SCRIPTURE I ♡ ↑

whatever is lovely

Where you
go I will ...

Psalms

JAMES

PETER

Mark

ruth

genesis

PROVERBS

Matthew

I will PRAISE YOU!

JOB

Esther

TIMOTHY

Mary

DAVID

ACTS

trinity

spirit

21154 Highway 16 East
Siloam Springs, AR 72761
Copyright © 2020 by Shanna Noel
All rights reserved.

Photo Credits: Lauren Norris, Jill Drangsholt, Addison Nalywaiko, Jaden Nalywaiko

Printed in Vietnam
Prime: J2439
ISBN: 978-1-64454-818-9